THE WONDERFUL WORLD OF WORDS

Queen Veronica Vanderbilt Verb

Dr Lubna Alsagoff

PhD (Stanford)

mc Marshall Cavendish
Children

Queen Veronica Vanderbilt Verb was the queen of verbs. She loved doing many things.

The queen loved to read.

Remember that verbs are doing words.

She loved to sing.

She loved to walk.

Most of all, she loved to drive fast cars!

The queen was very busy. She needed to make sure that everything and everyone in WOW did what they had to do.

She made sure that the tailors sewed new clothes.

She made sure that the carpenters built new houses.

She made sure that the artists painted beautiful pictures.

She made sure the bakers baked lovely loaves of bread.

5

The queen loved to have fun with the soldiers of WOW. She would order them to...

...stand very still,

...jump very high,

6

...run really fast.

And when the soldiers grew tired,
they simply fell to the ground,
and lay there, all in a pile!

crawl •

swing •

perch •

prance •

slither •

waddle •

swim •

hop •

Match the animal with the right verb to help it move!

8

Verbs can also name actions that people do.

When your nose feels tickly, you _____.

At night, you lay your head on your pillow and _____.

When you don't like something, you might _____.

When you are happy,
you _____.

Sometimes sad stories
make you _____.

When you are tired
or bored, you _____.

When you think something
is funny, you _____.

Play Snakes and Ladders with a friend.
Let's have some fun with verbs!

Stand on one foot **28**	**29**	Raise your right hand **30**	Cross your legs **31**
Rub your tummy **27**	Pinch your cheeks **26**	**25**	Close your eyes **24**
14	**15**	Wave with your left hand **16**	**17**
Wink at your friend **13**	**12**	**11**	Hop on one leg **10**
Start	**1**	Nod your head **2**	Bend your right elbow **3**

WOW

32	33	Finish

| | | Tap your feet |
| 23 | 22 | 21 |

| Bend and touch your toes | | Skip around the room |
| 18 | 19 | 20 |

| | | Shake your right leg |
| 9 | 8 | 7 |

| | Wiggle your toes | Shake your head |
| 4 | 5 | 6 |

What you'll need:
- 1 dice
- a counter for each player

How to play:
❶ Everyone takes turns.

❷ Roll the dice and move your counter.

❸ Do the action shown in the square you land in.

❹ If you land at the bottom of a ladder, climb it!

❺ If you land on a square with the head of a snake, slide down to its tail.

❻ The first one to reach FINISH wins!

13

Rabbit was worried.
He noticed more and
more of the animals
were not well.

So, Donkey, Owl, Squirrel and Rabbit set out to build a clinic. They had help from all the animals in the forest.

17

Everyone was proud of the clinic
when it was finally built.

And not long after that, there grew a
long queue of animals outside the clinic.
They all wanted to see Owl to get well.

Dear Grandma,

How are you? I hope you are enjoying trip your to Giant Ficus Trees the.

I wanted to tell you about things the strange that have been happening in forest the of WOW.

One day, we saw cloud purple a up in sky the, and after it rained, the all animals began to speak strangely. I am not sure if you can understand letter my because I, too, keep mixing up words my.

Please don't worry! Owl, Squirrel and Rabbit have come to help us. By time the you come home, we should all be well again.

Love,
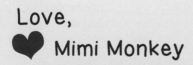 Mimi Monkey

Help Mimi's grandmother read the letter! Underline the words that are not in the right order, then write them in the correct order here. The first one has been done for you.

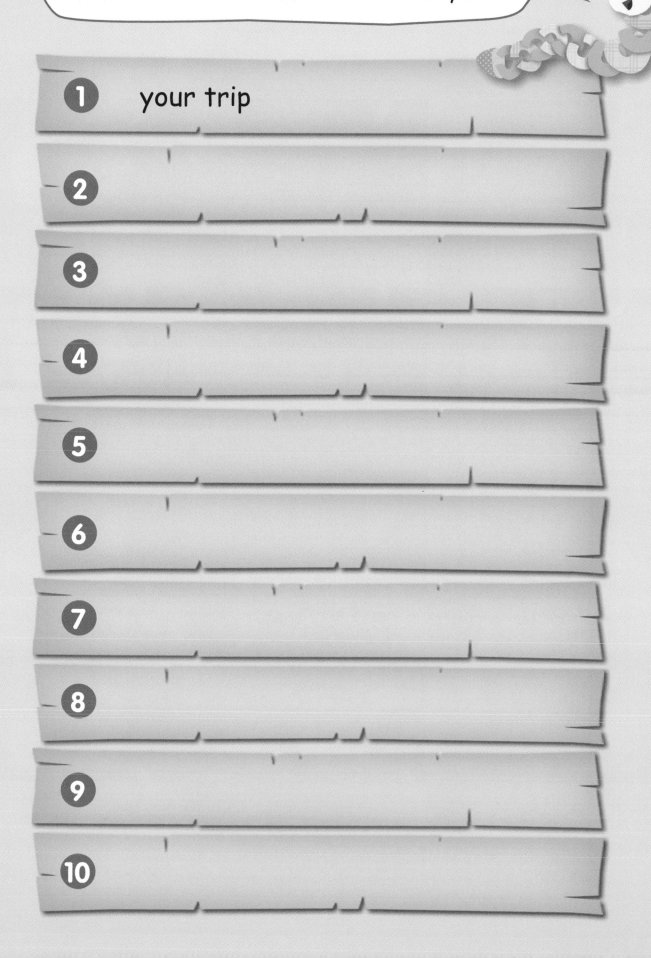

1. your trip

2.

3.

4.

5.

6.

7.

8.

9.

10.

Help the animals say things the right way.

You thank!

You are how?

Let help me you!

This is queue long a!

Can carry that I you for?

Long how will we have to wait?

22

I yesterday went to the bookstore.

She just now went to see the teacher.

I can buy what here?

I also must take my water bottle.

Remember to say your words in the right order!

23

Dear Parents,

In this issue, children should notice and learn:

- the different ways verbs are used to name actions.

- word order, and how words must be used in the correct position in a sentence.

Page	Possible Answers

8-9

ant → crawl   monkey → swing
frog → hop   deer → prance
snake → slither   duck → waddle
bird → perch   fish → swim

10-11

sneeze
sleep
frown
smile
cry
yawn
laugh

20-21

How are you? I hope you are enjoying **your trip** to **the Giant Ficus Trees**. I wanted to tell you about **the strange things** that have been happening in **the forest** of WOW.

One day, we saw **a purple cloud** up in **the sky**, and after it rained, **all the animals** began to speak strangely. I am not sure if you can understand **my letter** my because I, too, keep mixing up **my words**.

Please don't worry! Owl, Squirrel and Rabbit have come to help us. By **the time** you come home, we should all be well again.

22

Thank you!
How are you?
Let me help you.
This is a long queue.
Can I carry that for you?
How long will we have to wait?

23

I went to the bookstore yesterday.
She went to see the teacher just now.
What can I buy here?
I must also take my water bottle.

24